Faith in Action

Faith in Action

Studies in James

Mike Wilson

Spiritbuilding Publishing
Summitville, Indiana

Published by
Spiritbuilding Publishing
15591 N. State Road
Summitville, Indiana 46070

Printed in the United States of America

Unless otherwise indicated, Scripture citations are from The Holy Bible, English Standard Version, copyright © 2001 by Crossway Bibles, a division of Good News Publishers. Used by permission. All rights reserved.

Italics within Scripture quotations indicate emphasis added.

Page design, typesetting and cover by Hinds Design (www.HindsDesign.com).

Cover original artwork, *Presenting the Oil (James 5:14)*, by Brian Ward.

Wilson, Mike.
  Faith in Action: Studies in James / Mike Wilson.

www.SpiritBuilding.com

To Jay, my son-in-law

Contents

Favorite Sources

Rather than providing an exhaustive list of commentaries that went into preparing this booklet, I would rather note the following. They are personal favorites, most likely to be cited in the pages that follow. In some cases, their influence over the author is not expressly mentioned because, as someone has said, "Originality is the ability to forget where you got it."

Barclay, William. *The Letters of James and Peter* (The Daily Study Bible Series). Westminster, 1976.

Keener, Craig S. IVP *Bible Background Commentary: New Testament.* InterVarsity Press, 1993.

Loh, I-J. and Hatton, H. A. *A Handbook on the Letter from James* (UBS New Testament Handbook Series). United Bible Societies, 1997.

MacArthur, Jr., John. *The MacArthur New Testament Commentary.* Moody Press, 1983–2005.

Wiersbe, Warren W. *Be Mature: Growing Up in Christ.* Cook Communications, 2004.

By Way of Introduction
James 1:1

James is a picture book—"a series of pictures of what faith looks like—in the confronting of trial, in regard to speech and obedience to God's law, in response to gradations in people's social standing and to people in economic need, in the exercise of patience and prayer for the sick."

—Dictionary of Biblical Imagery

The Author: James

The New Testament contains many people named James, but only two of them are prominent enough to have written a book that begins, "James, a servant of God and of the Lord Jesus Christ." One of the two is James the son of Zebedee, brother of John, but he was executed too early to be seriously considered (Acts 12:2).

The other is James the Lord's brother, son of Joseph and Mary (Mt. 13:55; Mark 6:3). Midway through Jesus' ministry, James and his brothers were skeptics. John sadly reports, "For not even his brothers believed in him" (John 7:5). James and other family members apparently thought

Jesus was "out of his mind" (Mark 3:21, 31–35). Something changed, and this may have occurred after the resurrection. James was one of those to whom Jesus appeared as a risen Lord (1 Cor. 15:7). In any case, Jesus' brothers are among the band of believers in Acts 1:14. As time passed, James took on a leadership role within the Jerusalem church (Acts 12:17; 15:13–21), virtually on par with the apostles in influence (Gal. 1:19; 2:9; 1 Cor. 9:5). Later, he would meet with Paul in Jerusalem, with "all the elders" present (Acts 21:18–25).

According to Josephus, the high priest Ananus had James stoned to death (*Ant.* xx.9.1), an event that occurred around A.D. 62. The early Christian historian Hegesippus calls him "James the Just." He says that James had "camel" knees for his many prayers. He adds that eventually the Jews cast him down from a pinnacle of the temple and then stoned him to death (cited in Eusebius HE ii.23.3–18). Perhaps the writer of Hebrews had in mind James, among others, when he speaks of former leaders who "spoke to you the word of God. Consider the outcome of their way of life, and imitate their faith" (13:7). It is a testimony to James' widespread influence that Jude, another brother of the Lord, introduces himself as "a servant of Jesus Christ and brother of James" (Jude 1).

Recipients: the Twelve Tribes in the Dispersion

Normally the "dispersion" (or "diaspora") would refer to Jews living outside their homeland. The setting of this book is decidedly Jewish. James speaks of the "twelve tribes" (1:1), of a man coming into your "assembly" (lit. "synagogue," 2:2), and of rain patterns familiar to Palestinian Jews (5:7). However, a closer look at the message of James makes it clear that he is addressing *Jewish Christians*—those who hold their faith "in our glorious Lord Jesus Christ" (2:1). John MacArthur suggests that James' "primary audience

POWER POINT

Does any Christian feel completely at home in this world? We are living in what C. S. Lewis called "enemy-occupied territory." Wherever we may live, we are "dispersed."

were those Jews who had fled because of persecution and were still suffering trials because of their faith (1:2)." No one knows exactly when James was written, but many scholars now argue that this may be one of the earliest books of the New Testament and a vivid picture of still-predominant Jewish Christianity. One is tempted to think of the scattering of Jerusalem disciples after the persecution of Acts 8. Could it be that James was a communiqué to "beloved brothers" (1:16, 19; 2:5), formerly with him at Jerusalem, who were now "scattered because of the persecution" (Acts 11:19)?

The Channel of Communication: A Letter

A distinction must be made between *what* James says and *how* he says it—the manner of revelation. There are many literary devices by which God communicates his message in the Bible. Among them are law codes, historical reports, poems, dreams, visions, parables, curse formulas, songs, prophetic oracles, legal briefs, outbursts of praise, royal decrees, love stories, genealogical records, prayers, sermons, dirges, treaties, and role playing. These vehicles constitute the Holy Spirit's "delivery system."

God could have used other literary instruments. Some modern examples include dissertations, handbooks of rules and regulations, sales transactions, or certificates of grand prize eligibility. Even some of these elements are in the Bible—*e.g.*, sales transactions (*cf.* Jer. 32).

As is the case with many New Testament documents, the message of James is packaged in the form of a letter. What makes letters so special? For starters, God has allowed us to be snoopers, reading other people's mail! These little documents contain real-life people in real-life situations. They are more *personal* than other forms of communication.

Every society has its own conventions for letter-writing. This is not as prevalent in our society today, as the letters of Abraham Lincoln are much more formal than a modern email message. New Testament letters follow a conventional pattern that was familiar in that day and age:

- Author's name
- Recipient's name
- Greeting ("Grace and peace" was a Christianized phrase; James has the more common and generalized, "Greetings.")
- Prayer for the recipient's good health (missing in James)
- The main reason(s) for writing (sometimes underscored by, "I urge you...")
- Special salutations and personal greetings (which often contain the nuts and bolts of congregational life)

Even though James is a letter, parts of it read like a sermon ("Listen, my beloved brothers"—2:5). A modern reader listening to this master preacher can envision what it was like being in a first-century "assembly" (2:2). Other parts of James resemble the wisdom poetry of the Old Testament, especially the book of Proverbs (*cf.* James 3:13–18). James has been called "the Amos of the New Testament" because of his strong statements against social injustice (*cf.* James 5:1–6). Finally, there are strong parallels between the epistle of James and the Sermon on the Mount. Here are a few examples:

- Joy in trial (James 1:2; Mt. 5:10–12)
- Doers of the word, and not merely hearers (James 1:22; Mt. 7:21–27)
- Blessed are the poor (James 2:5; Mt. 5:3; *cf.* Luke 6:20)
- Adultery and murder (James 2:11; Mt. 5:21–22, 27–32)
- Mercy over judgment (James 2:13; Mt. 6:14–15)
- Dangers of the tongue (James 3:6; Mt. 5:22)
- Fruit of the mouth (James 3:10–12; Mt. 7:15–20)
- Friendship with the world is hostility toward God (James 4:4; Mt. 6:24)
- Judging (James 4:11–12; Mt. 7:1–5)
- Moth-eaten riches (James 5:2–3; Mt. 6:19–20)
- Oaths—do not swear (James 5:12; Mt. 5:33–37)

Outline of James
(a Preview of Future Lessons)

I. External Trials—1:2–12
a. A joyful heart—1:2
b. An understanding mind—1:3
c. A submissive will—1:4
d. An unwavering conviction—1:5–8
e. A humble spirit—1:9–11

II. A Contrast of Two Births—1:12–18
a. The birth of sin—1:13–16
b. The birth of a child of God—1:17–18

III. No Self-Deception Allowed—1:19–27
a. Receiving the Word—1:19–21
b. Implementing the Word—1:22–25
c. Living the Word—1:26–27

IV. Injustice in the Assembly!—2:1–13
a. The practice of injustice—2:1–4
b. The cure for injustice—2:5–9
c. The judgment on injustice—2:10–13

V. Faith without Works—2:14–26
a. Dead faith—2:14–20
b. Dynamic faith—2:21–26

VI. Controlling the Tongue—3:1–12
a. A universal problem—3:1–2
b. Little but powerful—3:3–6
c. Cannot be tamed—3:7–8
d. Blessing and cursing—3:9–12

VII. How to Gauge Wisdom—3:13–18
a. Worldly wisdom v. godly wisdom
b. The self-serving heart v. the servant heart

VIII. Man's Pleasure or God's Will? 4:1–12
a. What is the source of your problem? 4:1–3
b. Do you not know…? 4:4–6

  c. The remedy—4:7–10

  d. The cure realized—4:11–12

IX. "Come Now"—4:13–5:6

  a. To the entrepreneurs—4:13–17

  b. To wealthy landowners—5:1–6

X. The Triumphant Patience—5:7–12

  a. Be patient—5:7–8

  b. Do not complain—5:9

  c. Look at the examples—5:10–11

  d. Do not swear—5:12

XI. Spiritual Power—5:13–20

  a. Plugging into the right spiritual outlet—5:13–14

  b. The power of prayer—5:15–16

  c. Elijah: an example of the power of prayer—5:17–18

  d. The power to change an eternal destiny—5:19–20

REINFORCING THE LESSON

1. James calls himself a _____ of God and the Lord Jesus Christ. Everyone introduces himself in a certain way to others. It is the way we define and present ourselves to the world. How is James a powerful model in this regard?

2. The recipients of this letter are God's people who are "dispersed." In what sense are all Christians "sojourners and exiles" (1 Pet. 2:11)?

3. Letters are a powerful way to keep in touch and encourage brothers and sisters in Christ, both locally and abroad. Have you ever received a letter that impacted your life for good? Be prepared to share the experience with the class. And why not write a similar letter to someone else today?

4. Read the five chapters of James in one sitting. How long did it take you to read the whole epistle from start to finish? In your opinion, what is the main point of the book?

External Trials
James 1:2–12

Adversity forces us to focus on principles of scripture that will help us achieve spiritual victory and become more useful servants. We may see the reasons for it more clearly only in retrospect.
—*Christians and Cancer: A Journey of Hope*

THE FRENCH PHILOSOPHER Blaise Pascal said, "Being unable to cure death, wretchedness and ignorance, men have decided, in order to be happy, not to think about such things." It's an escape mechanism—*out of sight, out of mind*. Severe adversity is too depressing... so we fill our minds with diversions and create an imaginary world.

If you were to write the script of your own version of *It's a Wonderful Life,* would it include pain and suffering? We don't want to grow old, face adversity, or have to deal with life's inevitable problems. A good friend has a grandson who was consoling her about her age: "Grandma, you're not old; you just look really old!" The first paragraph of James is a reality check.

Ecclesiastes 12:13–14 teaches that life on earth is a probationary period, awaiting an ultimate day in court with the Almighty. This life is a test, and unforeseen challenges are part of the test. If we're crystal-clear on our purpose in life, we won't be totally blind-sided by them or discombobulated when they come. The moment we were born, we entered a battle zone, caught up in the crossfire of an age-old conflict (Rev. 12). There's a war going on, and there are going to be some casualties. We are not in a pain-free zone, but a war zone!

Consequently, we should expect some adversity, and it may come in all shapes and sizes:

- Severe illnesses
- Physical handicaps
- Financial crises
- Family problems
- Emotional trauma
- Relational problems
- Persecution
- Spiritual tests

Ultimately, there's a spiritual dimension to all these tests. Warren Wiersbe suggests that in the midst of trials on the outside (1:1–12) and temptations on the inside (1:13–27), there are three certainties: 1) we can be sure of the purpose of God (1:1–12); we can be sure of the goodness of God (1:13–18); and we can be sure of the word of God (1:19–27). In the first paragraph, James mentions five *coping mechanisms* in handling external trials.

A Joyful Heart (1:2)

"Count it all joy, my brothers, when you meet trials of various kinds…" The term for "trials" here was used of some *burden* or *threat* that constitutes either an inward temptation or an external "test" (*cf.* 1 Pet. 1:6–7).

> The corresponding verb is used of a young bird "testing" its wings, of "testing" drugs to see if they could cure diseases, of God "testing" Abraham to offer his son as sacrifice (Gen 22:1), of the Queen of Sheba "testing" the wisdom of Solomon (1 Kings 10:1), and so on. (USB NT Handbook)

Here is a great paradox: joy in the face of adversity! This is not the only time the Bible combines joy with trials. Jesus "for the *joy* that was set before him *endured the cross*" (Heb. 12:2). The apostles *rejoiced* "that they were counted worthy to *suffer dishonor* for the name" (Acts 5:41). Paul and Silas sang midnight hymns to the Lord in a jail cell (Acts 16:24–25). Jesus tells disciples that when persecution comes, "Rejoice in that day, and leap for joy, for behold, your reward is great in heaven; for so their fathers did to the prophets" (Luke 6:23). As a prisoner in Rome awaiting possible execution, Paul exclaims, "Rejoice in the Lord always; again I will say, Rejoice" (Phil. 4:4).

How can trials be faced with genuine joy, not in reluctant pretense? John MacArthur says,

> The more we rejoice in our testings, the more we realize that they are not liabilities but privileges, ultimately beneficial and not harmful, no matter how destructive and painful the immediate experience of them might appear. When we face trials with the attitude that James admonishes, we discover that the greatest part of the joy is drawing closer to the Lord—the Source of all joy—by becoming more sensitive to His presence, His goodness, His love, and His grace.

An Understanding Mind (1:3)

James continues: *"for you know that the testing of your faith produces steadfastness."* "For you know" indicates that a *joyful heart* is not the result of shallow enthusiasm, but it must be informed by an *understanding mind.* There is a depth of understanding behind the joy. A Christian *knows,* deep down, that the purpose of trials is to validate the genuineness of our faith (1 Pet. 1:6–7) and to build

POWER POINT

Peter Senge says, "Learning is highly contextual... It happens in the context of something meaningful and when the learner is taking action." Why is adversity such a powerful "classroom" for life's greatest lessons?

"steadfast endurance"—the ability to hold up rather than fold up when the pressure is on. Just as an athlete builds endurance through a stringent training regimen, external trials make us tougher and more resilient as our faith grows.

A Submissive Will (1:4)

The *"full effect"* of this steadfastness is *"that you may be perfect and complete, lacking in nothing."* "Perfect" means fully developed and mature. "Complete" implies that we are entire and whole. "Lacking in nothing" envisions the end result of a developmental process, of which affliction plays a big part. God's purpose, then, in allowing these trials is not to make us fall but to help us soar! As a potter with clay, he is molding us into *honorable vessels* (2 Tim. 2:21). Trials are one of the means he uses to eliminate our imperfections and get us refocused entirely on doing his will.

An Unwavering Conviction (1:5–8)

How can we find the "wisdom" to use these testing experiences in the right way? The answer is to pray for it. God will respond in two ways: "generously" and "without reproach." Wisdom is granted through the school of hard knocks, but it comes faster when accompanied by fervent prayer. God answers these requests by opening up our minds to appropriate words, actions, and opportunities that we did not see beforehand.

We must ask, then, "in faith, with no doubting." There must be a strong conviction that God is working with us through trials to build our character and put us in a better position to serve him. When we go to him praying for wisdom, then, we must pray with an absolute confidence that he will hear and respond. Our oldest daughter Megan once prayed during her little sister's illness, "Thank you for Brooke to get better." May we all have the childlike faith to see in advance God's answers to prayer. Jesus says,

"Truly, I say to you, whoever says to this mountain, 'Be taken up and thrown into the sea,' and does not doubt in his heart, but believes that what he says will come to pass, it will be done for him. Therefore I tell you, whatever you ask in prayer, believe that you have received it, and it will be yours" (Mark 11:23–24).

In fact, James likens the doubter to a "wave of the sea that is driven and tossed by the wind." That person is "unstable" and "double-minded"—literally a man with two souls or two minds on the inside. Obviously, God does not want us to be like the agnostic who prays, "God, *if there is a God,* save my soul, *if I have a soul,* from hell, *if there is a hell.*" We can do better than that.

A Humble Spirit (1:9–11)

The gospel brings to each person what he needs. To the poor man, it provides a new sense of his own value. He is "a brother for whom Christ died" (Rom. 14:15). As James asks elsewhere, "Has not God chosen those who are poor in the world to be rich in faith and heirs of the kingdom?" (James 2:5). Even the poverty-stricken are "loaded" with spiritual blessings in Christ!

The rich man, on the other hand, has a new sense of self-abasement. There is great peril in wealth, including the false sense of security it provides. Neither the rich or poor man should place much stock in material things, lest the cares, riches, and pleasures of life choke the Word (Luke 8:14).

POWER POINT

French philosopher Pierre Teilhard de Chardin remarked, "We are not physical beings having a spiritual experience, but spiritual beings having a physical experience."

The Reward

James concludes by saying, *"Blessed is the man who remains steadfast under trial, for when he has stood the test he will receive the crown of life, which God has promised to those who love him"* (1:12). A wise person once remarked, "He is no fool who gives what he cannot gain, to gain what he cannot lose."

1. Why do people play escapist games with regard to suffering? Is this healthy?

2. What are some types of adversity that Christians should expect in this life?

3. Restate the five *coping mechanisms* in handling external trials:

  ♦ A _____ heart (1:2)

  ♦ An _____ mind (1:3)

  ♦ A _____ will (1:4)

  ♦ An _____ conviction (1:5–8)

  ♦ A _____ spirit (1:9–11)

4. In light of our ultimate purpose in life, how can trials actually be beneficial?

A Contrast of Two Births
James 1:12–18

Most people who fly from temptation usually leave a forwarding address.

—Anonymous

"BLESSED IS THE *man who remains steadfast under trial…*" Verse 12 is a bridge between the consideration of external *trials* (1:2–12) and internal *temptations* (1:12–16). In this pivotal verse, one word (Greek *peirasmos*) does double duty. It refers to a *test* when the issue involves proving the good, and it means *temptation* when solicitation to evil is in view.

In this lesson, we will examine two pictures of birth: *1)* how sin is born (1:13–16); and *2)* how a child of God is born (1:17–18).

POWER POINT

What is the relationship between **trials of faith** and **temptations to sin**? Sometimes the difference lies in a person's response. For the Christian set on faithful obedience, the battleground is a trial that must be endured. For the one who succumbs to weakness, the same ordeal may be a launching pad for denying God. As Warren Wiersbe says, "If we are not careful, the testings on the outside may become temptations on the inside."

The Birth of Sin (1:13–16)

First, James argues that we cannot blame God for our sins: *"for God cannot be tempted with evil, and he himself tempts no one"* (1:13). The Greek *apeirastos* is literally "untemptable" (*Thayer*), i.e., without the capacity for temptation, or invincible to assaults of evil. The Bible says that God and evil exist in two incompatible realms. In Isaiah's heavenly vision, the prophet is struck with the words, "Holy, holy, holy is the LORD of hosts; the whole earth is full of his glory!" (Isa. 6:3). Habakkuk acknowledges, "You who are of purer eyes than to see evil and cannot look at wrong" (Hab. 1:13). Jesus is "holy, innocent, unstained, separated from sinners" (Heb. 7:26).

If sin is against God's nature, the thought that God could initiate a temptation with the intent of causing human sin is unthinkable. However, the idea is as old as Adam and Eve. The man indirectly blames God when he says, "The woman whom you gave to be with me, she gave me fruit of the tree, and I ate" (Gen. 3:12). Human beings have become masters at evasion when confronted with their guilt. Scottish poet Robert Burns captures it well:

POWER POINT

People minimize and redefine sin in less offensive terms, but, as B. Russell Holt says, "The object of all this verbal alchemy is to reduce sin from a felony to a misdemeanor, and the final goal is to get it off the books completely."

Thou knowest that Thou hast formed me
    With passions wild and strong;
And listening to their witching voice
    Has often led me wrong.

We can play the blame game, or dismiss personal evil as the byproduct of "the way we're made," but such attempts at displacement only prolong our self-deception (1 Jn. 1:8). Sinful humans are all too prone to remember the 11th Commandment: "Thou shall not get caught." Do you remember the two lines of poetry by Sir Walter Scott? "O what a tangled web we weave / When first we practice to deceive." Another writer added, "But when we've practiced quite a while / How vastly we improve our style!" To see who is responsible for our sin, we need only to look at the mirror.

How then does sin originate? *"But each person is tempted when he is lured and enticed by his own desire"* (1:14). "The metaphor is taken from hunting and fishing: as game is lured from its covert, so man by lust is allured from the safety of self-restraint to sin" (*Thayer*). The terms "lured" and "enticed" are used of the power of bait on fish.

Even though the enticement may be strong, it is one's "own desire" that gets the best of him. This means there is personal accountability for sin, and no passing of the buck is allowed. D. Edmond Hiebert says, "Temptation has its source not in the outer lure but in the inner lust." Thomas Adams adds, "Satan baits his hook according to the appetite of the fish." Someone has suggested that the whole person is involved in committing sin: intellect, emotions, and will. Intellectually, there is deception. Emotionally, there is desire. And volitionally, there is disobedience. All of these factors are highlighted by James: deception (1:14, 16), desire (1:14), and disobedience (1:15).

Sin is not an isolated act but the result of a specific process. A former professor of mine described it as LSD—*lust,* followed by *sin,* followed by *death* (Figure 1). James uses another analogy: *conception* and *birth.*

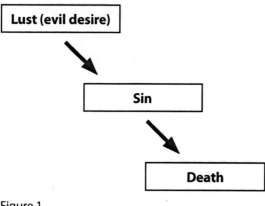

Figure 1.

"Then desire when it has conceived gives birth to sin, and sin when it is fully grown brings forth death" (1:15). The key to winning spiritual victory is *aborting* sinful desires, or, better yet, preventing their conception altogether.

Doug Barnett says, "If you don't want the devil to tempt you with forbidden fruit, you had better keep out of his orchard."

"Do not be deceived!" (1:16). God's "early warning system" is the conscience, which must be heard and not ignored. There is a battle in the mind or imagination, and sinful desire must not be allowed to move to the "planning" or "execution" stage. Spiritual "death" is not a trivial matter. There is no greater horror than separation from God.

The Birth of a Child of God (1:17–18)

James contrasts the birth of sin with the birth of God's children. First, he moves from evil to good: *"Every good gift and every perfect gift is from above…"* Sin taints and corrupts the world, but everything "good" is ultimately traceable to God. Even his commands are "for our good always" (Deut. 6:24). He is "the Father of lights," the one who made the sun, moon, and stars. The lights change, but not their Creator. With him "there is no variation or shadow due to change." Unlike astronomical imagery, revolving continually, there is a God whose character and goodwill toward us are constant.

This same God, who showers us with good things, has bestowed on us the ultimate gift. He has *"brought us forth by the word of truth, that we should be a kind of firstfruits of his creatures"* (1:18). James identifies four facts about the new birth:

- God has brought us forth. Christians are born into God's family (1 Jn. 2:29; 3:9).

- This is done, James says, "of his own will"—*i.e.*, in keeping with the plan that God himself has executed and set into motion (John 1:12–13).

- The tool by which this new birth is accomplished is "the word of truth," or the gospel (*cf.* 1:21; 1 Pet. 1:23).

- Finally, the end result of this birthing process is that God makes his people a kind of "firstfruits," *i.e.*, sacred to God as his special property (Deut. 18:4–5; Jer. 2:3).

REINFORCING THE LESSON

1. A blessing is pronounced on the one who passes the test (1:12).
   What is the ultimate promise for those who are victorious?

2. Why are people prone to blame their sins on God? (1:13)

3. Disease often represents a complete breakdown of the body's
   immune system, but medical procedures sometimes treat the
   symptoms and not the cause. How does James treat the underlying root cause of sin? (1:14–15)

4. How does Jesus do the same thing with "murder" (Mt. 5:21–22)
   and "adultery" (Mt. 5:27–28)?

5. Victory over sin means interrupting the "process" before it
   fully develops. What are some of the "tools" God has given us
   to win the victory?

6. The Bible is full of "success stories" in the battle against sin.

   ◆ What strategy did Joseph use? Gen. 39:13

   ◆ What strategy did Job use? Job 31:1

   ◆ What strategy is recommended in Proverbs 4:14–15?

   ◆ What strategy did Jesus use? Mt. 4:4, 7, 10

   ◆ What strategy did Jesus recommend to the disciples?
     Mt. 26:41

   ◆ What strategy is found in James 4:7?

Lesson 3—A Contrast of Two Births (James 1:12–18)

7. In keeping with James' description of the birth of God's children (1:18)...

 ◆ Into what are they born? _____

 ◆ This is done according to God's _____

 ◆ The tool that brings it about is the _____

 _____

 ◆ The end result is that God's people are a kind of _____

 _____

No Self-Deception Allowed
James 1:19–27

Judgment Day finally arrived. The voice of the archangel shouted and the trumpet of God sounded. Suddenly, there was an appearance of a great white throne. There were people everywhere—from every culture, race, and language, and from every period of human history. And there was one man waiting his turn with nervous confidence. After all, Jesus was his Lord and he had done many mighty works in Jesus' name. But the events of that day took a sudden and unexpected turn. When his time came, there was a terrible feeling that overwhelmed him as he heard the pronouncement, "I never knew you; depart from me, you who practice lawlessness."

cf. Matthew 7:21–23

I N THE LAST section of James 1, the emphasis is on self-deception as we hear and apply God's Word. James 1:22 says, "But be doers of the word, and not hearers only, *deceiving yourselves.*" Verse 26 continues, "If anyone thinks he is religious and does not bridle his tongue *but deceives his heart,* this person's religion is worthless." Consequently, Warren Wiersbe prefaces this section, "Quit Kidding Yourself." We follow the line of thought in three stages:

- Receiving the Word—1:19–21
- Implementing the Word—1:22–25
- Living the Word—1:26–27

Receiving the Word (1:19–21)

In the parable of the sower (Luke 8:4–15), Jesus compares God's word to seed and the human heart to soil. Here James uses the same metaphor: the "implanted word." In Jesus' parable, there are four types of people who respond to the gospel:

1. the hard heart (pathway soil);
2. the shallow heart (rocky soil);
3. the divided heart (thorny soil); and
4. the fruitful heart (good soil).

If the word of God does not bear fruit in a changed life, then there is something deficient or inadequate in our hearts as we receive it. How then should we receive the word?

"Be quick to hear" (1:19). As Jesus said, "He who has ears to hear, let him hear" (Mt. 13:9). No one should follow in the steps of Nabal, who was "such a worthless man that one cannot speak to him" (1 Sam. 25:17). The classical writer Zeno said, "We have two ears but only one mouth, that we may hear more and speak less." A tribute was once paid to a great linguist because he could be silent in seven different languages. Unfortunately, though, some people do not listen well. When it comes to the reception of God's truth, most erroneous interpretations start with someone who is not paying careful enough attention to what the text actually says.

"Slow to speak." Many of the Old Testament Proverbs warn against hasty use of the tongue. "When words are many, transgression is not lacking, but whoever restrains his lips is prudent" (Prov. 10:19); "Whoever guards his mouth preserves his life; he who opens wide his lips comes to ruin" (Prov. 13:3); "Even a fool who keeps silent is considered wise; when he closes his lips, he is deemed intelligent" (Prov. 17:28); "Do you see a man who is hasty in his words? There is more hope for a fool than for him" (Prov. 29:20). This principle is true in human relations generally, but it is especially true when it is time to listen to God's word. Could it be that the "quarrels" and "fights" mentioned later in James 4:1 were the result of brothers speaking up too quickly?

"Slow to anger." Again, this is a theme familiar to Old Testament wisdom literature. "Whoever is slow to anger has great understanding, but he who has a hasty temper exalts folly" (Prov. 14:29). Warren Wiersbe says,

> When the Prophet Nathan told King David the story about "the stolen ewe lamb," the king became angry, but at the wrong person…In the Garden, Peter was slow to hear, swift to speak, and swift to anger—and he almost killed a man, with the sword. Many church fights are the result of short tempers and hasty words.

There is such a thing as righteous indignation, but "man's anger does not produce the righteousness that God requires" (1:20). Wiersbe adds, "Like the man who broke the mirror because he disliked the image in it, people rebel against God's Word because it tells the truth about them and their sinfulness."

With a prepared heart (1:21). The human heart is like a garden that needs to be weeded and cultivated. James urges us to pull out the weeds and prepare the soil for the "implanted word." This is reminiscent of Jeremiah, who said, "Break up your fallow ground, and sow not among thorns" (Jer. 4:3). There are two things to yank out or "put away." *"Filthiness"* reminds us that sin makes people dirty, and we have to clean up our hearts. *"Rampant wickedness"* ("superfluity of naughtiness," KJV) is depravity. Jeremiah 17:9 says, "The heart is deceitful above all things, and desperately sick; who can understand it?" Precisely because of the human tendency toward corruption, we must make every effort to clean up our hearts and receive the message of salvation "with meekness."

Implementing the Word (1:22–25)

"But be doers of the word, and not hearers only, deceiving yourselves" (1:22). Hearing a good sermon does not necessarily make people stronger spiritually. Rather, it is the *doing* and not the *hearing* that brings a blessing (1:25). James compared the word of God to seed, but now he

changes the analogy. It is also a mirror. As we look at the mirror, we see ourselves as we really are. "Mirror, mirror on the wall, who's the fairest of them all?" We're not!

Just as people take a superficial look at themselves in the bathroom mirror, and forget to make changes to their appearance, a cursory reading of the Bible will never reveal our deepest needs. We have to take a much closer look. Wiersbe says, "It is the difference between a candid photo and an x-ray."

"But the one who looks into the perfect law, the law of liberty, and perseveres, being no hearer who forgets but a doer who acts, he will be blessed in his doing" (1:25). Application of divine truth takes time, reflection, and meditation (Ps. 1; 119:97).

Slipshod Bible study cuts corners, and the mirror is not used properly. Fruitful study is hard work. It takes time, and there are no shortcuts. It requires the attitude in the "search warrant" psalm: "Search me, O God, and know my heart! Try me

> **POWER POINT**
>
> In Bible study, there are three steps to self-discovery and internalization:
>
> **Observation** — what does the text say?
>
> **Interpretation** — what does it mean?
>
> **Application** — how can I apply it to my life?

and know my thoughts! And see if there be any grievous way in me, and lead me in the way everlasting!" (Ps. 139:23–24).

Living the Word (1:26–27)

"If anyone thinks he is religious…" (1:26). "Religious" means that one is "careful of the externals of divine service" (Vine). However, there is more to faithful Christianity than outward ceremony. God wants more than a mechanical ritual. What makes a man or woman a true Christian? We have to get beneath the surface. When application of the Word becomes a *life pattern*, our whole lives begin to impact others.

We begin to think like a "servant" (1:1).

James focuses on speech (1:26), service (1:27), and separation from the world (1:27). In *speech*, one must "bridle his tongue," an idea more fully developed in 3:1–12. However outwardly pious one may appear at times, if he does not control the tongue, his influence for good will be curtailed.

In *service*, there are widows and orphans to visit. "Religion" is not a substitute for deeds of love (1 Jn. 3:16–18; James 2:14–17; John 13:12–15). The visitation of "orphans and widows in their affliction" demands personal involvement—*i.e.*, the requirement is not satisfied by sending a few dollars to an institution from a comfortable distance. What are we doing to touch the lives of others who need it most? What are you doing to help the helpless? In benevolence, evangelism, and hospitality, a Christian's barometer of care and concern for others is demonstrated in the degree of personal involvement he is willing to invest.

Then there is *separation from the world.* The "world" here is "society without God." James 4:4 urges us not to be *friends with* the world. 1 John 2:15 tells us not to *love* the world. Romans 12:2 commands us not to be *conformed to* this world. Here in James 1:27, we are urged to be "unstained" from the world—*i.e.*, unspotted or unblemished. The world will leave its mark on you if you allow it. Like a tattoo, it won't easily wash off.

Separation from the world is not total alienation. Wiersbe says,

> It is not necessary for the Christian to get involved with the world
> to have a ministry to the world. Jesus was "unspotted" (1 Pet. 1:19),
> and yet He was the friend of publicans and sinners.

Receiving the Word (1:19–21), implementing the Word (1:22–25), and living the Word (1:26–27) must be done without self-deception. Jesus says, "Not everyone who says to me, 'Lord, Lord,' will enter the kingdom of heaven, but the one who does the will of my Father who is in heaven" (Mt. 7:21). Judgment Day is coming. The stakes are too high to be a hearer and not a doer.

REINFORCING THE LESSON

1. Self-deception is a big problem when it comes to the hearing and application of divine truth (1:22, 26). Give an example of one way people lull themselves into a false sense of security after studying the Bible.

2. How can the admonition, "Be quick to hear, slow to speak, slow to anger," apply to the way in which we receive the Word? 1:19

3. Why is it important to clean up the heart as a condition of receiving the implanted Word? 1:21

4. What image does James use to illustrate the hearer who is not a doer? 1:22–24

5. What terms does James use to describe God's law? 1:25

6. What are the three applications James makes in the area of living the Word in 1:26–27?

   ✦

   ✦

   ✦

Injustice in the Assembly!
James 2:1–13

They came together to worship God as brothers and sisters in Christ but walked away from the meeting place with this sick feeling in their guts. Something just wasn't right. People were not treating each other as Christians should. Instead of feeling better because of the assembly, they felt worse. Is this a 21st-century scenario? No, it is a page right out of James in the first century!

THE EPISTLE OF James contains a priceless snapshot of early Christianity. Then, as now, disciples were less than perfect and needed to be corrected. This is especially evident in the second chapter, where James allows us to take a peek at blatant sin in the church assemblies. People can act like *people* in any century. That's what makes this so relevant. The key is not to pretend that we are something we're not but to span the gap between what we are and what we ought to be.

The Practice of Injustice (2:1–4)

James first tells his readers how *not* to practice the faith: *"My brothers, show no partiality as you hold the faith in our Lord Jesus Christ, the Lord of glory"* (2:1). Jesus had a humble birth. Unlike foxes and birds, he had no certain home. He did not have the right education, money, or other trappings of greatness. And yet because of what he accomplished and the position he now occupies, we recognize the Lord Jesus as glorious. He alone is "the Lord of glory."

The rest of us (in the church) are brothers and sisters in Christ. We have attained this position because of what Jesus did for us. Apart from him, no Christian possesses anything of lasting value. Consequently, social posturing has no place in the church.

James goes on to give a caricature. *"For if a man wearing a gold ring and fine clothing comes into your assembly, and a poor man in shabby clothing also comes in, and if you pay attention to the one who wears the fine clothing and say, 'You sit here in a good place,' while you say to the poor man, 'You stand over there,' or, 'Sit down at my feet,' have you not then made distinctions among yourselves and become judges with evil thoughts?"* (2:2–4). In Roman society, distinctions in social rank were a part of daily life. There were senators, equestrians, soldiers, farmers, slaves and freedmen. A senator would wear a toga with a purple stripe and a "gold ring." Among prominent Jews, there was a pecking order concerning where to sit at a wedding feast (Luke 14:7–11) as well as *the best seats in the house* at the synagogue (Mt. 23:6). This human depravity for partiality was oozing into the church. The poor man was being despised.

POWER POINT

It's better to speak honestly and openly about what can (and does) happen in the church rather than sweep it under the rug. We are not perfect—as individuals or congregations—but we can be transparent and honest. Unbelievers will more likely appreciate authenticity in us than false pretensions. And when we model our efforts after first-century Christianity, we are trying to follow a perfect blueprint, not the imperfections of people who embraced it.

The Cure for Injustice (2:5–9)

James next goes on to the antidote for such misconduct.

1. Recognize the objects of true wealth. *"Listen, my beloved brothers, has not God chosen those who are poor in the world to be rich in faith and heirs of the kingdom, which he has promised to those who love him?"* (2:5). The "faith of our Lord Jesus" is an endowment (2:1; *cf.* 1:9). God has overturned the social scales and given true wealth to the impoverished. In the kingdom, even the poor man is "rich."

2. Think about how your actions dishonor the have-nots. *"But you have dishonored the poor man"* (2:6)—and this, a brother "for whom Christ died" (Rom. 14:15).

3. Consider how despicable the unbelieving "rich" really are. *"Are not the rich the ones who oppress you, and the ones who drag you into court? Are they not the ones who blaspheme the honorable name by which you were called?"* (2:6–7). These are people who exploit others, who control the levers of carnal power, and who blaspheme Christ's name. What kind of role model is that? Do you really want to be like *them?*

4. Ponder the law that holds you accountable. James saves the most important argument for last: *"If you really fulfill the royal law according to the Scripture, 'You shall love your neighbor as yourself,' you are doing well. But if you show partiality, you are committing sin and are convicted by the law as transgressors"* (2:8–9). Even though the specific "law" cited was first expressed in the Old Testament period (Lev. 19:18), it is fundamental to everything God has *always* wanted from his people. The requirement is "second" in importance only to loving God with every fiber of our being (Mt. 22:36–40). All other ethical laws in Scripture flow out of these two. As such, the requirement cited is truly a "royal law" because it is integral to "the kingdom of heaven."

The Judgment on Injustice (2:10–13)

No law is good unless it has teeth. Built into God's law is the ultimate system of accountability. *"For whoever keeps the whole law but fails in one point has become accountable for all of it"* (2:10). How can that be?

"For he who said, 'Do not commit adultery,' also said, 'Do not murder.' If you do not commit adultery but do murder, you have become a transgressor of the law" (2:11).

Notice first that God's law is a perfect expression of the one who gave it. James does not introduce verse 11 with, "For *that which* said..." but "For *he who* said." Our attitude toward the law reflects our attitude toward God.

Second, "adultery" and "murder" are easy-to-see examples of a more insidious problem—the injustice of partiality. The context hasn't changed: *"So speak and so act as those who are to be judged under the law of liberty. For judgment is without mercy to one who has shown no mercy. Mercy triumphs over judgment"* (2:12–13). When we are guilty in this life of injustice, it will not be *justice* that we ourselves seek on Judgment Day, but *mercy*—the same mercy that we must extend to the outcast brother who needs our affirmation.

Finally, the law that will judge us is a "law of liberty." It is a law that frees us in several ways. It inhibits harmful activity, liberates us from guilt, and enables even the poor man to be "rich in faith." Most of all, in this context especially, it releases us to practice mercy toward one who is judged harshly by the standards of this world.

If someone of great worldly importance were to walk into the building where you assemble for worship, how many people would trip over their feet to meet this celebrity, while bypassing a lowly "nobody"? How often do people play cruel games, devising subtle ways of putting others in their place? Do power, skin color, prestige, or money factor into your assessments of others? May God help us rid our minds of such prejudices so that we can act mercifully. The Judge is waiting!

POWER POINT

Imagine a funny-looking kid who is the butt of everyone's jokes in school. Someone must befriend him and show him the Savior's love. The "law of liberty" frees the tender-hearted Christian to do what Jesus would do.

REINFORCING THE LESSON

1. The following scenario really happened. A local church has a number of young couples. Some of them like to socialize together, and they refer to themselves as "the A-group." They ostracize the others and call them "the B-group." What should happen now?

2. James gives a caricature of the wealthier brother telling the poor man where to sit (2:2–4). Reality is usually more subtle, and people act without thinking how their behavior hurts others. What are some ways, consciously or unconsciously, in which the in-crowd can promote a feeling of entitlement among themselves, while putting others in their place?

3. What designation does James use to call himself in 1:1, and what are the implications for this lesson?

4. What are some positive things we can do to promote healthy relationships in the church?

Faith without Works
James 2:14–26

Believing and *doing* are blood relatives.

—*S. Rutherford*

"*F*AITH WITHOUT WORKS *is dead.*" Some expositors have walked a tightrope with James 2. On the one hand, they acknowledge with James that one's faith cannot be lifeless or inactive. However, in deference to their theology, they cannot admit that this is a salvation issue. John MacArthur reveals his evangelical bias when he says that James "was not dealing with the means of salvation at all, but rather with its outcome, the evidence that it had genuinely occurred." Consequently, a popular explanation among evangelicals is that we are justified *before God* by faith alone, and we are justified *before men* by the works of faith that they can see.

That's not exactly what James says. When speaking of faith in the absence of works, James asks, "Can that faith *save* him?" (2:14). Whatever else may be said of James' contrast, this is definitely a salvation issue.

Martin Luther, the Protestant reformer who championed "faith alone" theology, relegated the letter of James to second-class status, calling it "an epistle of straw...for it has nothing of the nature of the gospel about it." Bible students with an axe to grind have attempted to explain away the second chapter of James ever since.

In this section, James first gives illustrations of dead faith (2:14–20); then he moves to dynamic faith (2:21–26).

Dead Faith (2:14–20)

Confession without obedience (2:14). John MacArthur rightly says, "The genuineness of a profession of Jesus Christ as Savior and Lord is evidenced more by what a person does than by what he claims. A person who professes Christ but who does not live a Christ-honoring, Christ-obeying life is a fraud." Jesus taught the same thing (Mt. 7:21). As the vine to the branches, he warns that "every branch of mine that does not bear fruit he takes away" (John 15:2). Warren Wiersbe says, "People with dead faith substitute words for deeds. They know the correct vocabulary...and can even quote the right verses from the Bible; but their walk does not measure up to their talk." Words are not enough.

Compassion without benevolence (2:15–17). A verbal concern for those in need can be nothing more than a hypocritical sham (*cf.* Mt. 25:31–41, 45). In the story of the Good Samaritan, both the priest and the Levite had pretensions of religious allegiance, but neither of them paused to assist a dying man on the roadside (Luke 10:25–39). If we see a need and offer a few pious words, in the language of James, "what good is that?" As John says, "But if anyone has the world's goods and sees his brother in need, yet closes his heart against him, how does God's love abide in him? Little children, let us not love in word or talk but in deed and in truth" (1 John 3:17–18).

Conviction without compliance (2:18–20). True saving faith involves something that others can see and recognize: a changed life. The daily affirmation of godly Jews was, "Hear, O Israel: The LORD our God, the LORD is one" (Deut. 6:4). James says, "You believe that God is one; you do well." But a verbal conviction is not enough. He adds that even the demons share this faith.

People are surprised to hear that demons believe in God. There are evidently no atheist demons. They believe that Jesus Christ is the Son of God (Mark 3:11–12). Their faith is more than intellectual conviction, causing them to "shudder." That is more faith than a lot of human beings have. Yet even if someone has faith equal to that of the demons, he can be enlightened in mind and stirred in heart, and still be lost.

Inactive faith is "dead" (vv. 17, 26) and "useless" (v. 20). It is unproductive and idle. Like the barren fig tree, it bears no fruit. It is a counterfeit faith that lulls a person into false confidence about his salvation.

Dynamic Faith (2:21–26)

Dynamic faith, by contrast, is living, vibrant, and active. There are three components of Biblical faith: a) conviction of mind; b) trust of heart; and c) surrender of the will. Whereas dead faith touches only the intellect and possibly the emotions, dynamic faith encompasses the intellect, the emotions, and the will. The heroes of faith in Hebrews 11 were people of action. "By faith Abel offered... By faith Noah constructed an ark... By faith Abraham obeyed." Through faith, they acted valiantly and with courage. Someone has said, "Faith is not believing in spite of evidence; faith is obeying in spite of consequence." (Wiersbe)

James then illustrates this principle in the lives of two well-known people from the Old Testament. Abraham was a Jew and Rahab was a Gentile. Abraham was a righteous man and Rahab was a sinner, a prostitute. Abraham had been a man of faith for many years, whereas Rahab was brand new at the business of serving God. One might say that Rahab was justified by faith in the God of heaven for the first time, while Abraham's justification was an ongoing process. The obedience of saving faith is not an isolated event. It starts when a person first comes to God and it continues through life.

Abraham (2:21–24). In Genesis 15:5–6, God challenges Abraham to count the stars. He then promises him, "So shall your offspring be." Verse 6 says that Abraham "believed the LORD, and he counted it to him as righteousness." "Counted" is a financial or commercial term. It means to credit one's account. In a manner of speaking, God symbolically deposited righteousness into Abraham's spiritual bank account. Abraham was counted a righteous man because of his faith in God's promise.

Probably at least 25 years later, in Genesis 22, Abraham passes the ultimate test of faith—the offering of Isaac on the altar. When his faith was tested to such an extreme degree, he obeyed, his faith reached its peak, and his justification became full and complete. Prior to this, God declared him righteous, but this declaration was provisional, conditioned on the severe test he would have to pass. When Abraham's faith was shown to be equal to the test, his justification was fully realized, and he would be called the friend of God (2 Chron. 20:7; Isa. 41:8). James 2:23 says that the earlier passage in Genesis was "fulfilled" when Abraham's faith became complete. The one scripture about God counting Abraham righteous was "fulfilled" about a quarter of a century later when he passed this test. James 2:22 says Abraham's faith "was active along with his works." Verse 24 adds, *You see that a person is justified by works and not by faith alone.*

Rahab (2:25–26). Another lesser-known Old Testament hero, she received the spies sent to Jericho and helped them escape. Her heart had been convicted about the truth of God (Josh. 2:8–13). She did something about her convictions. In fact, she risked her own life to save these two men. Should not such faith be rewarded? It was a faith that did something bold and daring.

The Bottom Line

Some people react violently to the idea that salvation involves "works"— even works that are an outgrowth of our faith. Perhaps it is helpful to look at the different kinds of "works" in the Bible:

- Works of the flesh (Gal. 5:19, 21)
- Works of the devil (1 John 3:8)

◆ Works of the Law of Moses (Gal. 2:16)

◆ Works of personal merit (Eph. 2:8–9; Titus 3:5)

◆ Evil works (Col. 1:21)

◆ Dead works (Heb. 9:14)

None of these works will save anybody.

However, "works of faith" are in a very different category.

◆ Remembering before our God and Father your *work of faith* and *labor of love* and steadfastness of hope in our Lord Jesus Christ (1 Thess. 1:3).

◆ For in Christ Jesus neither circumcision nor uncircumcision counts for anything, but only *faith working through love* (Gal. 5:6).

◆ For as the body apart from the spirit is dead, so also *faith apart from works is dead* (James 2:26).

A faith that does not work is a faith that does not save. When we first come to Christ, our faith must translate into action, as there are conditions that must be met (Acts 2:37–38, 41). As we walk with God, our faith must continue to act, just like Abraham's did!

REINFORCING THE LESSON

1. Is "faith without works" a salvation issue? 2:14

2. Inactive faith is _____ (vv. 17, 26) and
_____ (v. 20).

3. According to the breakdown in this lesson, dead faith encompasses...

   ◆ Confession without _____ (2:14)

   ◆ Compassion without _____ (2:15–17)

   ◆ Conviction without _____ (2:18–20)

4. Contrast Abraham and Rahab. What do they have in common? How are they different? 2:21–16

5. What are the components of dynamic faith?

   ◆ _____ of mind

   ◆ _____ of heart

   ◆ _____ of will

6. How does one respond to the idea that "works" do not affect a person's salvation?

Bonus Lesson: "Altar Call Salvation"

ONE THING THAT differentiates those who profess Christianity is an understanding of when salvation occurs. When exactly does a person become a Christian? For Roman Catholics and some Protestants, infant baptism is part of the formula, and it's validated later on in a rite called *confirmation,* when the child is old enough to "confirm" the decision his parents already made for him. For many Evangelical Protestants, the rite of passage is sometimes referred to as the "altar call" or the "sinner's prayer."

Evangelicals are highly influenced by the theology of Martin Luther and also the camp revivals of the early 1800s. Consequently, their understanding of the dividing line is summarized as "salvation by faith alone." Since baptism is usually not regarded by them as part of the process, the whole idea of baptism as a requirement for salvation seems preposterous. There's a lot of emotional investment tied to *dehydrating* the new birth, based on preconceived notions of how salvation is attained.

What Does the Bible Teach?

The Acts of the Apostles is the only inspired work of history that records actual cases of conversion in the apostolic church. It contains sermon excerpts detailing what inspired preachers taught to lost souls. There are many examples of how lost men and women responded to this preaching—*i.e.*, what they actually did when the sermons were over.

A consistent pattern emerges. Consider just a few of the many examples:

- And Peter said to them, "Repent and be baptized every one of you in the name of Jesus Christ for the forgiveness of your sins, and you will receive the gift of the Holy Spirit." (Acts 2:38)

- But when they believed Philip as he preached good news about the kingdom of God and the name of Jesus Christ, they were baptized, both men and women. (Acts 8:12)

- And as they were going along the road they came to some water, and the eunuch said, "See, here is water! What prevents me from being baptized?" (Acts 8:36, 38–39)

- And he took them the same hour of the night and washed their wounds; and he was baptized at once, he and all his family. (Acts 16:31–34)

- "And now why do you wait? Rise and be baptized and wash away your sins, calling on his name." (Acts 22:16)

That pattern involves a process:

- Hearing the gospel
- Believing in Jesus
- Repenting of past sins
- Confessing Jesus publicly
- Being baptized

Baptism is the only requirement besides faith that consistently comes up over and over. It is mentioned more frequently in these cases of conversion than repentance. It is "for the forgiveness of sins"

(Acts 2:38). It was done immediately in response to gospel preaching. It brought great joy (*cf.* Acts 8:39). People were happy because through baptism their sins were forgiven and they now had a relationship with God through Jesus Christ.

On the other hand, the "altar call" and "sinner's prayer" are conspicuously absent from the New Testament. They just are not there!

Where Then Did "Altar Call" Theology Come From?

It did not happen overnight. There was a long process of change through church history. Christians in the earliest centuries consistently linked baptism to salvation. Consider the following examples from the second century.

- We descend into the water full of sins and uncleanness, and we ascend bearing reverence in our heart and having hope in Jesus in our spirit. (*Epistle of Barnabas,* 11:11)

- "I have heard, Sir, from some teachers that there is no other repentance except that one when we descended into the water and received the forgiveness of our former sins." He said to me, "You heard correctly, for it is so." (*Shepherd of Hermas,* Mandate 4.3.1)

- As many as are persuaded and believe that the things taught and said by us are true and promise to be able to live accordingly are taught to fast, pray, and ask God for the forgiveness of past sins, while we pray and fast with them. Then they are led by us to where there is water, and in the manner of the regeneration by which we ourselves were regenerated they are regenerated. For at that time they obtain for themselves the washing in water in the name of God the Master of all and Father, and of our Savior Jesus Christ, and of the Holy Spirit. For Christ also said, "Unless you are regenerated, you cannot enter the kingdom of heaven..." (Justin Martyr, *Apology* 1.61)

◆ It has assuredly been ordained that no one can attain knowledge of salvation without baptism. This comes especially from the pronouncement of the Lord, who says, "Except one be born of water he does not have life." (Tertullian, *On Baptism* 12)

In later church history, baptism came to be regarded as a sacrament. Infants were baptized in light of the false idea that they were somehow born in sin and needed to be cleansed. Sprinkling replaced immersion as the mode of baptism. There was little personal investment in the conversion process. After all, a baby cannot believe, repent of sins, or give his body as a living sacrifice. Roman Catholics further corrupted things by developing an entire system of salvation based on personal merit and human works.

As is so often the case in church history, the pendulum that had swung too far in one direction ended up swinging too far in the other. Martin Luther and the Protestants fought one extreme by going too far to the other extreme. He knew that the Catholic idea of meritorious works had to be wrong, as no one can earn his salvation. He read in the book of Romans that salvation was by faith. Even though he held to the necessity of infant baptism, his theology revolved around salvation by "faith alone." This paved the way for baptism to be regarded by Protestants as something not connected to salvation, something done after the fact—*i.e.*, nothing but "an outward sign of an inward grace."

The camp meetings and revivals of the early 1800s provided a new twist that solidified modern evangelical practice. They lasted for several days and were marked by considerable emotional display. The first significant one of the period was held in 1800 in Logan County, KY. The most famous camp meeting was in 1801 at Cane Ridge in Bourbon County, KY, directed by Barton W. Stone, and attended by 25,000 people. Stone later saw baptism as part of the conversion process and in fact became one of the leaders of the Restoration movement.

About 1830, a fiery preacher named Charles Finney perfected the "altar call." What he called the "anxious seat" came to be called the "mourner's bench." In the 20th century, Billy Graham employed his version of the altar call "invitation" followed by the "sinner's prayer" and "receiving Christ into your heart." The peculiarities of the evangelical "invitation" to salvation grew out of these types of developments, associated with revivals and crusades. According to Fred Zaspel, a Baptist, the altar call "first arose more than eighteen centuries after Christ." According to David Bercot, an evangelical who converted to Anglicanism, "The altar call and associate prayers are a product of the revival movements of the eighteenth and nineteenth centuries, and they were unknown to any Christians before that time."

What About Bible Passages Teaching Faith Without Works?

For example, Romans 4:1–5 teaches that God justifies the one who has "faith" and not the "one who works." A number of theologians have imposed a meaning on Paul's contrast which is totally foreign to it. In the case of Luther, it was through the prism of his own struggle against Catholic error that he misunderstood Paul.

The contrast is not between effort and no effort, action versus inaction, or external obedience versus internal faith. We should not read something into this that is not there.

In Romans 4, Paul is saying that there are only two paths to a right relationship with God, which he calls "faith" and "works." Both paths involve effort, but Paul is discussing the parameters that define the effort. On the one hand, "works" implies human performance rendered so perfectly that there is no sin, no need of salvation, and no need of a Savior.

This road is forever blocked by our own sin (Rom. 3:23). We cannot earn a ticket to heaven on our own merit. The only other option is to place our trust in someone who makes forgiveness possible, to have faith in the Savior who has made provisions for human failure.

Some have seen a contradiction between Romans 4 and James 2 on faith and works. James 2:24 says, "You see that a man is justified by works, and not by faith alone." It is interesting that the only verse in the Bible which puts the words "faith" and "alone" together says that salvation is *not* by "faith alone."

Does James 2 contradict Romans 4? No! In Romans 4, Paul is condemning a kind of works that precludes the need for faith and of salvation. James, on the other hand, is denouncing a kind of faith that precludes the need for works. Another way of looking at this is that the "works" in the two passages involve two different things. In Romans 4, Paul is saying that the provision for a relationship with God is not supplied with human effort. *I.e.*, we cannot achieve this on our own. In James 2, James speaks of the acceptance of the provision supplied by someone else. *I.e.*, we must be active, not passive, in receiving God's saving grace and living a life of faith.

Even in Romans, where Paul denounces "works" as a system of self-justification before God, he is not against an active obedience. In this same epistle he speaks of "the obedience of faith" in the opening lines (Rom. 1:5) and of "obedience of faith" in the closing lines (Rom. 16:26). In the heart of the book, he says, "But thanks be to God that though you were slaves of sin, you became obedient from the heart to that form of teaching to which you were committed" (Rom. 6:17). This obedience, which is part of our faith in Christ, includes baptism (Rom. 6:3–4).

Faith, broadly understood, involves three components: 1) Conviction of mind; 2) Trust of heart; and 3) Surrender of the will. Does "faith alone" save? *No!* The devil has messed up people's thinking, and there is a huge emotional investment in perpetrating a false doctrine. When we teach them the truth on this issue, we may have to show extraordinary patience.

REINFORCING THE LESSON

1. What is the only book in the Bible that records actual cases of conversion in the early church?

2. There is a pattern of conversion found in the New Testament. Give scriptural evidence for the steps that it involves.

3. Where did the modern evangelical "altar call" originate?

4. What is the only verse in the Bible to put "faith" and "alone" together?

5. A friend argues that Romans 4:1–5 teaches that salvation is available by *faith alone*, apart from anything we do, including baptism. How would you respond?

Controlling the Tongue
James 3:1–12

Words are like nitroglycerine: they can keep a heart ticking, or
they can blow up a bridge!   —*Anonymous*

W ARREN WIERSBE CALLS the tongue "the world's small-
est but largest troublemaker." There is an old adage:
"Sticks and stones may break my bones, but words
will never hurt me." Unfortunately, that is not always
the case. Words can hurt! There is one letter that separates *"word"* from
"sword."

It's not hard to tarnish someone else's reputation or undermine his
influence for good. A few fiery darts in the back should do the job very
nicely. This is a problem addressed frequently in the Bible. In 1 Samuel
24:9, David asks King Saul, "Why do you listen to the words of men,
saying, 'Behold, David seeks to harm you'?" Read Psalm 55:2–3, 6,
12–14, 21–22. The Psalmist is saying, in essence, "He was a smooth
talker, but he stabbed me in the back!" Fortunately, the final verses of
the psalm take comfort in God's promise to sustain the faithful at such
times (Ps. 55:22–23).

A Universal Problem (3:1–2)

Teachers, beware! (3:1) Some jobs are perilously risky. Not everyone should become a teacher because those who occupy a formal teaching position must master the use of a potentially hazardous tool. Not just anyone can learn how to properly use the tongue. There is the danger of hypocrisy, of saying one thing but doing another (Rom. 2:19–24). Another danger is carelessness. On at least one occasion, the apostle Peter opened his mouth without realizing what he was saying (Luke 9:33). By sticking to the text of divine revelation, teachers can stay out of a lot of trouble (1 Pet. 4:11), but it is easy to make off-the-cuff statements that are not supported by the truth.

> ### POWER POINT
>
> As the story goes, during his last year in office, Winston Churchill attended an official ceremony. Several rows behind him two gentlemen began whispering. "That's Winston Churchill."
>
> "They say he is getting senile."
>
> "They say he should step aside and leave the running of the nation to more dynamic and capable men."
>
> When the ceremony was over, Churchill turned to the men and said, "Gentlemen, they also say he is deaf!"

A peril for all people: *"We all stumble in many ways"* (3:2). It's not just teachers who are in jeopardy. "Stumble" here is literally to slip up or trip. Lord Fisher said, "Life is strewn with orange peels." James adds that a "perfect man" is one who "does not stumble in *what he says*"—i.e., through the use of his vocal cords. Man is by his very nature a creature of verbal communication, but there is inherent peril in opening the mouth.

Little But Powerful (3:3–6)

A horse's bridle (3:3). Little things often make a big difference. *"If we put bits into the mouths of horses so that they obey us, we guide their whole bodies as well."*

A ship's rudder (3:4). "Strong winds" drive a ship, but a "very small rudder" determines the pathway it takes.

A small flame (3:5). Several years ago, a *Smokey the Bear* ad said, "One tree can make 3,000,000 matches. One match can burn 3,000,000 trees." A tiny spark can destroy a great forest. One over-zealous commentator went so far as to say, "There is no divine law which the tongue cannot break."

Cannot Be Tamed (3:7–8)

"Every kind of beast" can be and has been tamed, but *"no human being can tame the tongue."* If you have ever been to an animal show at Sea World or a wild animal park, you have witnessed the taming of animals. Why is it that the tongue is so difficult to conquer? There are so many ways it can get us into trouble. The list would include:

- Lying (Rev. 21:8)
- Cursing (Job 2:9)
- Gossip (Rom. 1:29–30)
- Slander (Prov. 20:19)
- Boasting (Prov. 27:2)
- Filthy talk (Eph. 5:4)
- Rage (James 1:19)

Is anyone totally innocent of all these and other sins of the tongue?

Blessing and Cursing (3:9–12)

Blessing the Lord (3:9). With the tongue *"we bless our Lord and Father."* God blesses us when he bestows on us a temporal or spiritual gift. As priests of God, we bless other people when we invoke the favor of God upon them (*cf.* Num. 6:24–26; 2 Tim. 4:22). We bless God when we give him the glory, honor, and thanksgiving that he deserves. "Bless the LORD, O my soul, and all that is within me, bless his holy name!" (Ps. 103:1). "So I will bless you as long as I live; in your name I will lift up my hands" (Ps. 63:4). As Cecil F. Alexander's poem, *All Things Bright and Beautiful,* says,

He gave us eyes to see them,
　And lips that we might tell
How great is God almighty,
　Who has made all things well.

Cursing men (3:9). With the same tongue *"we curse people who are made in the likeness of God."* James continues, *"From the same mouth come blessing and cursing. My brothers, these things ought not to be so"* (3:10).

The inconsistency (3:10–12). James goes on to paint several word pictures showing the hypocrisy of it all.

- Does a spring pour forth from the same opening both fresh and salt water?
- Can a fig tree bear olives?
- Or a grapevine produce figs?
- Neither can a salt pond yield fresh water.

As Christians, we need to unleash the power of speech for good. There is always plenty of room for encouragement, humble correction, confession of our faith in Christ, thanksgiving, and praise.

REINFORCING THE LESSON

1. Should Christians aspire to be teachers? Does James 3:1 contradict Hebrews 5:12? What is the real point of James 3:1?

Lesson 8—Controlling the Tongue (James 3:1–12)

2. James gives three illustrations of little things that pack a big wallop (3:3–6). List them:

   ◈

   ◈

   ◈

3. Why is the tongue so difficult to "tame"? 3:7–8

4. What is wrong with the same mouth *blessing God* and *cursing men*? 3:9–12

5. How can gossip be stopped?

55

6. List some examples of destructive speech.

7. Give some examples of wholesome speech.

How to Gauge Wisdom
James 3:13–18

It is better to get wisdom than gold. Gold is another's, wisdom
is our own; gold is for the body and time, wisdom for the soul
and eternity.
—Matthew Henry

AMES NOW MOVES from the control of the tongue to a compari-
son of two kinds of wisdom. A lot of people are "street smart"
and "wise to the ways of the world." Godly wisdom is something
else entirely.

Who is Wise and Understanding? (3:13)

Wisdom and understanding. *"Who is wise and understanding among you?"*
I.e., who is "wise" in that wisdom that is divine in nature and origin?
"Understanding" describes the expert or learned one. In the context,
such wisdom and expertise are the hallmarks of one who is capable
and qualified to teach (v. 1).

Good behavior. *"By his good conduct let him show his works..."*
A self-proclaimed wise man isn't necessarily wise. Even in the church—or

57

especially in the church—not just anyone should be promoted to a position of responsibility. There is a standard of excellence and a level of proficiency that must be attained (*cf.* 1 Tim. 3:10; Luke 16:10; 2 Tim. 2:2). Only those who have proven themselves with a reliable track record of "good conduct" should be appointed to positions of responsibility.

In the meekness of wisdom. "Meekness is the opposite of arrogance. It is often understood as self-effacement or submissiveness and is therefore considered by many as a weakness rather than a virtue" (UBS NT Handbook Series). However, in the Bible it is an attribute of those who have a deep inner strength (*cf.* James 1:21; 2 Tim. 2:24–26; Mt. 5:5). It is humble concern as opposed to self-will, a lack of pretentiousness, and the ability to work with people. It describes a person who is *wise as a serpent* and *innocent as a dove* (Mt. 10:16).

False Wisdom (3:14–16)

Two manifestations. False wisdom is characterized by "bitter jealousy" and "selfish ambition." It is the spirit of rivalry that poisons otherwise good people and destroys healthy relationships (Phil. 1:15–18; James 4:1–6).

Misses the mark. False wisdom is off target because it does two things. It *boasts* and it *lies* (against the truth).

Its source. Its origin is demonic (v. 15). It is "not from above." Rather, it is diabolical. It is...

- Earthly (versus heavenly)
- Natural (versus spiritual)
- Demonic (as opposed to God and his holy angels)

Its results. The outcome of false wisdom is "disorder and every vile practice." This is a picture of chaos and malpractice. How can people accomplish anything good together if they are steaming with envy? Truly, "a house divided cannot stand."

True Wisdom (3:17–18)

The "wisdom from above" is identified by the following traits. These are the "fingerprints" it leaves behind:

- ◈ *Pure*—innocent and clean
- ◈ *Peaceable*—not factious
- ◈ *Gentle*—considerate, equitable, fair and mild
- ◈ *Open to reason*—"In general it describes someone whose mind is not closed, who is not insistent but always willing to listen to other people's views and ready to be persuaded." (UBS NT Handbook Series)
- ◈ *Full of mercy*—see James 2:13
- ◈ *Full of good fruits*—the "outcome of their way of life" is evident (Heb. 13:7; *cf.* James 3:13; 1 Pet. 2:15; 2 Cor. 8:21)
- ◈ *Impartial*—without dubiousness or ambiguity in doing right; unwavering
- ◈ *Sincere*—literally, without hypocrisy

Finally, James adds, *"And a harvest of righteousness is sown in peace by those who make peace"* (3:18). The strongest barrier to godly wisdom is a heart motivated by self-interest. Envy and jealousy carry a toxic impact that clouds a person's thinking and pollutes healthy relationships. Earthly wisdom will even sneak into churches and create havoc. On the other hand, those who attain "wisdom from above" will develop a *servant-heart* rather than a *self-serving heart*. The proof of this wisdom, James says, is in the "harvest of righteousness...sown in peace." The two models are contrasted in Figures 2 and 3 below.*

---

* Figure 2 is modified from a more extensive chart in Blanchard and Hodges, *Lead Like Jesus*, p. 49.

Worldly Wisdom

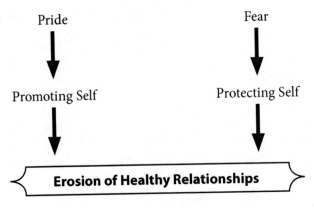

Figure 2.

Godly Wisdom

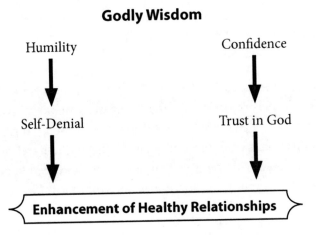

Figure 3.

1. Much of this section is reminiscent of Proverbs in the Old Testament. Proverbs also deals with the source of true wisdom.

✦ Prov. 1:7—The _____ of the LORD is the beginning of knowledge; fools despise wisdom and instruction.

✦ Prov. 9:10—The fear of the LORD is the beginning of _____, and the knowledge of the Holy One is insight.

2. What problems does worldly wisdom produce?

✦ James 3:16. _____

✦ James 4:1. _____

✦ James 4:4. _____

3. James says worldly wisdom is "demonic" (3:15). Does that mean demons still operate in the world? *Cf.* 1 Tim. 4:1

4. Worldly wisdom is *self-centered,* and godly wisdom is *God-centered.* What can happen when one strong-minded element in a local church operates on the basis of worldly wisdom, and another operates with godly wisdom?

5. Application: in order to change the focus from worldly wisdom to godly wisdom, one must...

  ◆ Be brutally honest in examining his motives

  ◆ Pray (James 1:5)

  ◆ Listen...humbly (James 1:21)

  ◆ Develop a God-centered orientation in which...

    » Humility replaces pride

    » Confidence in the Lord replaces fear

  ◆ Promote a transparency that fosters authentic relationships with God and others

How well are *you* doing in developing and applying the "wisdom from above"?

Man's Pleasure or God's Will?

James 4:1–12

Worldliness is rampant in the church. The devil is not fighting churches, he is joining them! He isn't persecuting Christianity, he is professing it.

—Vance Havner

I N THIS SECTION James addresses the basic question of whether our aim in life is to submit to God or to satisfy our own worldly pleasures. If worldly gratification is the policy of life, then nothing but hatred and strife can possibly follow. The long, drawn-out resentments which result are like "wars." At various junctures of the epistle, James touches on several types of potential disagreements:

◆ Class conflicts (2:1–9)

◆ Church fights (3:13–18)

◆ Personal vendettas (4:11–12)

◆ Labor wars (5:1–6)

What is the Source of Your Problem? (4:1–3)

The problem: "quarrels" and "fights." Conflict is never easy. James gets to the origin or root cause.

The diagnosis: "passions" that wage "war." There is not enough church in the world, and too much world in the church. "Passions" (or "pleasures") comes from the same root that gives us the word, *hedonism*, and means "sensual delights."

- **You lust.** James says that because worldly desires are not fulfilled, *"so you murder."* Human beings are in competition for worth and value. One has more, and another has less. Murder, even in a symbolic sense, is the removal of a rival (*cf.* Mt. 5:21–22). This is what prompted the first homicide (Gen. 4:3–8).

- **You covet.** Envy leads to desire for what others have—and a sense of emptiness when those desires are not personally realized. *"So you fight and quarrel."*

- **You do not have, because you do not ask.** When people are consumed by material things, prayer is not high on the agenda.

- **When you do ask, you ask in vain.** James likely addresses *have-nots* (*cf.* 2:6–7), who might have been tempted to "spend it on [their] passions" (or "pleasures"). Selfish motives lead to unanswered prayers.

Do You Not Know? (4:4–6)

One commentator calls this a "confident inquiry." James elaborates on the diagnosis, driving the point home.

Friendship with the world is enmity with God. In fact, so severe is the breach of trust that James uses the term, "adulteresses." Just as murder in this context is metaphorical (v. 2), so James draws on familiar imagery from the Old Testament prophets to brand worldly Christians with the guilt of adultery (see 2:11 for a similar pairing of "murder" and "adultery"). The reason for the feminine, "adulteresses," is that spiritual adultery is ultimately against Israel's rightful husband, God (*cf.* Ezek.

16:25, 30, 32, 37, 41; Jer. 3:1, 3, 8–10). In the Old Testament passages, Israel forsakes the LORD to commit adultery with forbidden lovers (*i.e.*, false gods). In this passage, the forbidden love is "the world." "Friendship with the world" is "hostility" toward God. The wedge is so deep that the offender becomes God's "enemy."

God yearns for us. *"Or do you suppose it is to no purpose that the Scripture says, 'He yearns jealously over the spirit that he has made to dwell in us' "*? (4:5). This is one of the most difficult sayings in James. He is probably not citing a specific Old Testament scripture—only the general principle taught throughout the Bible that God's "jealousy" makes an exclusive claim on human loyalties (*cf.* Ex. 20:5; 34:14; Zech. 8:2).

God is opposed to the proud but gives grace to the humble. When James speaks of *"more grace"* (or "greater grace") in verse 6, the point may be that "God's grace is more than adequate to meet the requirements of his jealousy," in spite of the magnitude of man's sin (UBS NT Handbook Series). Or James may be saying that God's grace is greater than anything this sinful world has to offer (*cf.* v. 4). The statement, *"God opposes the proud, but gives grace to the humble,"* comes from the ancient Greek translation of Proverbs 3:34, not from the original Hebrew (which accounts for the slight differences in wording). The "grace" that we all desperately need to cure us from our sinful infatuation with the world is available only to "the humble."

The Remedy (4:7–10)

Submit to God. "Submit" is a military term, and it means to put oneself under the authority of another. Enmity with God was achieved through rebellion, but his grace can only be attained through submission (*cf.* 1 Pet. 5:5–9).

Resist the devil. When God's people "stand against" or "withstand" the devil, *"he will flee from"* them. He will "turn and run" (REB).

Draw near to God. God himself "will draw near" to those who draw near to him. When the prodigal son came home, his father ran to meet him (Luke 15:20).

65

Cleanse ... purify ... humble yourselves. *"Cleanse your hands, you sinners; and purify your hearts, you double-minded. Be miserable and mourn and weep; let your laughter be turned into mourning and your joy to gloom. Humble yourselves in the presence of the Lord, and he will exalt you"* (4:8b–10). If someone wants to know what repentance looks like, this is it!

The Cure Realized (4:11–12)

Do not speak against one another. If worldly passions produce "quarrels" and "fights" in the church (v. 1), then humility and repentance lead to brotherly love (*cf.* 1 Pet. 5:5). "Love covers a multitude of sins" (1 Pet. 4:8). There is no room for gossip and slander, which are against the "royal law" that includes loving one's neighbor as oneself (James 2:8).

God is the only Lawgiver and Judge ... able to save and destroy. Isaiah 33:22 says, "For the LORD is our judge; the LORD is our lawgiver; the LORD is our king; he will save us." The United States Constitution calls for three branches of government. In heaven's government, God holds absolute prerogative in all three domains:

◆ *Legislative:* "there is only one lawgiver"

◆ *Judicial:* "and [only one] judge"

◆ *Executive:* "he who is able to save and to destroy" [*i.e.*, only one king]

If this is so, then mere humans are not in a position to "judge the law" (on slander or anything else). Our task is not to judge but to comply.

Lesson 10—Man's Pleasure or God's Will? (James 4:1–12)

1. Why is it so important to get to the underlying causes of conflict in the church?

2. In what ways is God's grace an effective antidote to infatuation with the world?

3. What is the four-step remedy for worldliness that James offers in vv. 7–10?

    ⦿

    ⦿

    ⦿

    ⦿

4. What is the relationship between respect for God and a loose tongue?

"Come Now"
James 4:13–5:6

"... And he who earns wages does so to put them into a bag with holes."
—*Haggai 1:6*

C RAIG KEENER, an expert in New Testament-related cultural issues, takes a novel approach to the Epistle of James. He believes James is addressing Jewish Christians caught up in social tensions that eventually produced the Jewish War of A.D. 66–70. James died about A.D. 62, but in the years leading up to the war, Jewish Zealots took advantage of widespread social unrest and started a revolution. Keener says,

In the first century, many peasants worked as tenants on larger, feudal estates (as elsewhere in the empire); others became landless day laborers in the marketplaces, finding work only sporadically (more was available in harvest season). Resentment against aristocratic landlords ran high in many parts of the empire, but nonpayment of promised goods to them was hardly an option; a few landowners even had their own hit squads of hired assassins to deal with uncooperative tenants.

Christians were caught in the crossfire of these social currents. This background of fermenting social revolution paints a more specific picture of the "lowly brother" of 1:9; the "poor man in shabby clothing" (2:2); the brother or sister who is "poorly clothed and lacking in daily food" (2:15); the great forest "set ablaze by such a small fire" (3:5); the contrast between "demonic" wisdom versus the "wisdom from above," which is "peaceable, gentle, [and] open to reason" (3:13–18); the seduction of "friendship with the world" (4:4); and even the fighting, quarreling, and murder of 4:2. In Keener's view, "James addresses here many of the poor, the oppressed, who are tempted to try to overthrow their oppressors and seize their goods."

According to Keener, James 4:13–5:6 now shifts attention to the wealthy crowd, in contrast to the oppressed classes: *i.e.*, those with *new money* (4:13–17) and *old money* (5:1–6). He says,

> Most of the wealth in the Roman Empire was accumulated by one of two means: the landed gentry, of high social class, made their wealth from land-based revenues such as tenant farmers and crops; the merchant class gathered great wealth without the corresponding social status. James addresses both merchants (4:13–17) and the landed aristocracy (5:1–6). (*IVP Bible Background Commentary*: NT. Electronic Edition: PC Study Bible)

James begins both paragraphs with the two-word challenge, "Come now…" (4:13; 5:1). Those are "fightin' words."

To the Entrepreneurs (4:13–17)

Big plans for the future (4:13). James addresses merchants who say, *"Today or tomorrow we will go into such and such a town and spend a year there and trade and make a profit."* Jewish entrepreneurship has deep-seated roots.

No guarantees (4:14). *"Yet you do not know what tomorrow will bring. What is your life? For you are a mist that appears for a little time and then vanishes."* The one certainty about the future is its uncertainty. Moreover, life passes by so quickly. Truly, "The years of our life are seventy, or even by reason of strength eighty; yet their span is but toil and trouble; they are soon gone, and we fly away" (Ps. 90:10).

Instead, you ought to say, "If the Lord wills..." (4:15). As the rich fool learned (Luke 12:20–21), we are not ultimately masters of our own destiny. "Do not boast about tomorrow, for you do not know what a day may bring" (Prov. 27:1).

No room for arrogance (4:16). Earthly goals should be provisional and tentative, and they ought to be qualified with the sentiment, "Lord willing." The assumption of unlimited time and opportunity amounts to a false boast.

No room for procrastination (4:17). Since we are operating on God-given time, then the most important business—*spiritual things*—should receive top priority. *"So whoever knows the right thing to do and fails to do it, for him it is sin."*

To Wealthy Landowners (5:1–6)

Prophetic taunt. The tone is reminiscent of the Old Testament prophets, who often took up a "dirge" in mockery of a self-inflated world power (*cf.* Isa. 13:6–7; 14:4, 9). Jesus occasionally does the same thing (*cf.* Luke 10:13–15).

Earthly wealth doesn't last (5:1–3). Riches rot, garments are eaten by moths, and precious metals rust. Misery is coming! Many of the original recipients of this letter were poor (1:9–10; 2:5–6), and James' summons to "weep and howl" is a comforting thought for have-nots suffering oppression by the well-to-do.

Injustices will be repaid (5:4–6). Upper class corruption is nothing new. We shudder when ordinary folks lose everything while an investment manager walks away with a multi-million dollar severance package. James speaks of those who have fattened themselves and withheld pay from the little guy. The Lord knows what is going on, he hears the outcry of the oppressed, and a day of reckoning is coming!

Summary

Financial concerns will always be front-page news on earth. Honest people need to make a living, corruption will follow the trail of big money, and politicians will issue endless calls for economic reform. Ultimately, our lives should not be about money. In the bigger scheme of things, it is just a tool which serves a temporary purpose. For those who think otherwise: *"Come now...!"*

REINFORCING THE LESSON

1. According to the view presented in the lesson, who are the two classes of people James addresses in this segment?

    ◆ _____ (4:13–17)

    ◆ _____ (5:1–6)

2. Is it wrong to develop a financial plan? If not, then what are some spiritual components which should be built into it?

3. Is there a place for a prophetic-style taunt in a culture obsessed with political correctness? What purpose does the taunt serve in James 5:1–6?

The Triumphant Patience
James 5:7–12

Patience must not be an inch shorter than affliction.

—*Thomas Adams*

WE LIVE IN a pressure-cooker world...where dangerously heavy weights of anxiety hang on the threads of patience. Competition requires high-level performance. Stress peaks every few days. Tempers flare. Stomachs turn. Ulcers bleed. Hearts break. Nerves unravel. Minds blow. Some drop out.

Myth #1 is that if you're a Christian, you won't have any problems. Myth #2 is that being exposed to Bible teaching will automatically solve all your problems. If the preceding section warns entrepreneurs and condemns the selfishly rich, this paragraph gives comfort to brothers in need of patience. Four times James uses the term, "brothers," as he admonishes and encourages them (vv. 7, 9, 10, 12).

Be Patient (5:7–8)

"Until the coming of the Lord." We cannot be preoccupied with this life. The ultimate example of patience is farming. The farmer must wait for the early and late rains (*cf.* Joel 2:23).

It is not our nature to be patient, and some people think patience is for losers and failures—for those who take the long view because success in the short term eludes them. Notice that it is often the achiever who tells the less-than-achieved to be patient, and how patronizing it sounds. The person learning a new skill is told, "Be patient. It will come." Peter Gomes suggests that patience implies passivity, and we don't want to be passive, merely spectators at somebody else's achievement. We want to be proactive, to get on with it, to make things happen. "No one gets anywhere by being patient, right?"

Most of us live in an urban society, but there's something you need to know about the farmer. He is anything but a passive participant in the process. Farmers who do not work hard are usually not very successful. A good farmer realizes two things: 1) The harvest is the result of incredible patience; and 2) The harvest is the result of really hard work.

James is not necessarily writing to farmers. Whether or not the original recipients were accustomed to using their hands, they were certainly held hostage to disillusionments in their minds. What comfort does James bring to them? What is the harvest for which we wait? It is nothing less than the return of the Lord Jesus. *Strengthen your hearts! Jesus is coming! The Lord's coming is "at hand."*

What does James mean? Was he mistaken? Is he crying wolf? For starters, we must understand that the Lord is on a different time clock than we are (2 Pet. 3:8–10). It may not seem so, but *the Judge is standing right at the door* (v. 9). If that was true in the first century, it is certainly true today! Jesus is not slumbering or taking a nap. Therefore you should strengthen your hearts and be ready to welcome him when he returns (*cf.* 2 Tim. 4:7–8).

Do Not Complain (5:9)

In time of pressure, tempers fly. For example, when there is a family crisis, it's easy to become irritable. People lash out or play the "blame" game. Little things become big things, blown completely out of proportion. The Judge is "standing at the door" and is "ready to judge the living and the dead" (1 Pet. 4:5). For that reason, we had best not grumble and complain against each other. It would be a terrible thing for a Christian to lose his salvation because of uncontrolled anger and an unbridled tongue.

POWER POINT

The Value of Waiting

There are four great benefits to developing patience in our daily walk:

- **We learn to depend on God as never before**—a tremendous blessing! "Waiting on God" forces us to rely on him, not on ourselves.

- **We learn what a relationship with God is worth.** As in all healthy relationships, if every detail were neat and tidy, life would be really boring and predictable. God wants to enter genuine give-and-take relations with you, so that you have a real two-way relationship. There are going to be unexpected twists and turns, but these will allow you to get closer to God

- **When we have to wait on God, we gain a greater appreciation of how long he has waited for us.** The Lord has waited for his wayward children to repent, and he waits with extraordinary patience for them to get busy in his service. When it comes to the waiting game, God will outlast us every time.

- **When we have to wait, we begin to grasp his love for us all the more.** The better the prize, oftentimes the longer we have to wait—and we will appreciate it more if we have to wait. Instant gratification is rarely a good thing. You've heard the expressions, "Anything worth having is worth waiting for"; or "The best things come to those who wait." Waiting on God always has a happy ending!

Look at the Examples (5:10–11)

The Bible is stuffed full of examples of real people. As an example of suffering and patience, *consider the prophets*. Jeremiah, full of despair, accuses God of deception, because the prophet had "become a laughingstock all the day" and "everyone mocks me" (Jer. 20:7). He even cursed his own birthday, wishing he had never been born (20:15–18). Yet when duty called, Jeremiah could not contain himself: "If I say, 'I will not mention him, or speak any more in his name,' there is in my heart as it were a burning fire shut up in my bones, and I am weary with holding it in, and I cannot" (Jer. 20:9).

Hebrews 11:32–40 says,

> And what more shall I say? For time would fail me to tell of Gideon, Barak, Samson, Jephthah, of David and Samuel and the prophets—who through faith conquered kingdoms, enforced justice, obtained promises, stopped the mouths of lions, quenched the power of fire, escaped the edge of the sword, were made strong out of weakness, became mighty in war, put foreign armies to flight. Women received back their dead by resurrection. Some were tortured, refusing to accept release, so that they might rise again to a better life. Others suffered mocking and flogging, and even chains and imprisonment. They were stoned, they were sawn in two, they were killed with the sword. They went about in skins of sheep and goats, destitute, afflicted, mistreated—of whom the world was not worthy—wandering about in deserts and mountains, and in dens and caves of the earth. And all these, though commended through their faith, did not receive what was promised, since God had provided something better for us, that apart from us they should not be made perfect.

What great role models! We have a tremendous heritage of heroes who have gone before us. Consider Job, a great man who lost everything but his faith. Job reminds us of another myth—that if you are having problems, then you must be unspiritual. On the contrary, God was allowing this righteous man to endure a test. James speaks of the "purpose of the Lord," or outcome of the Lord's dealings, since in spite of everything Job has a happy ending. If we endure like Job, we too will experience compassion and mercy (*cf.* Rom. 15:4; Heb. 13:8).

Do Not Swear (5:12)

He's not talking about cursing, though other passages would condemn that (*cf.* James 3:9; Lev. 24:11). The issue here, as in the Sermon on the Mount (Mt. 5:33–37), is frivolous oath-taking. Jesus says that it would be better to simply say "Yes" or "No" than engage in Pharisaical games of truth or dishonesty (*cf.* Mt. 23:16–22). *I.e.*, let your word be your bond, even without the extra assurances of an oath formula.

James gives a reason not to swear: *"so that you may not fall under condemnation."* This admonition seems entirely out of place. What does swearing an oath have to do with heavenly patience? If you have ever suffered, you know the answer. In the middle of a severe crisis, in the heat of the moment, it is tempting to say things one does not mean, or even strike a bargain with God. Do you remember Jephthah's foolish vow (Judg. 11)? It cost him a daughter!

Going back to Job, when he was challenged by his wife to "curse God and die," he said,

> "Naked I came from my mother's womb, and naked shall I return. The LORD gave, and the LORD has taken away; blessed be the name of the LORD." In all this Job did not sin or charge God with wrong. (Job 1:21–22)

Summary

It *is* a pressure-cooker world, especially for Christians. We will have trials and tribulations. How does one overcome? Success is a result of committing your soul to a faithful Creator, not complaining about your brethren, looking at heroes of faith who've gone before us, and waiting patiently for the coming of the Lord.

REINFORCING THE LESSON

1. What can the farmer teach us about patience?

2. List four benefits of learning to "wait" in the face of adversity:

   ◈ _____

   ◈ _____

   ◈ _____

   ◈ _____

3. What does complaining about our problems accomplish?

4. What can the prophets teach us about "suffering and patience"?

5. Why is the example of Job such a powerful testimony to the value of staying power?

6. What does "swearing" have to do with the rest of the lesson?

Spiritual Power
James 5:13–20

"God heals, and the doctor takes the fees." —*Benjamin Franklin*

ECOND TIMOTHY 3:5 CONTAINS a sad description of those whose spiritual life is nothing but a hollow shell: *"having the appearance of godliness, but denying its power."* James 5:13–20 is the polar opposite. It contains the formula for tapping into the real power of the Christian life. In some ways, it is a commentary on Ephesians 3:20—*"Now to him who is able to do far more abundantly than all that we ask or think, according to the power at work within us…"*

Plugging Into the Right Spiritual Outlet (5:13–14)

James saves some of his best material for last. This is perhaps the most practical teaching in an application-rich treatise. It reminds us that the Word of God is not a heavenly fog but a down-to-earth reality. James mentions three conditions of life, and then he offers the appropriate spiritual outlet for each.

Is anyone among you suffering? Let him pray. "Suffering" is literally "to suffer evil," hence to undergo hardship or distress. The corresponding noun is applied to the prophets of old in verse 10. Troubling affliction should not be bottled up on the inside. Spiritual release and divine help are found in prayer. Truly, Christians are to "pray without ceasing" (1 Thess. 5:17).

Is anyone cheerful? Let him sing praise. True worship covers the whole gamut of human emotion. There are not only moments of grief but moments of intense joy and euphoria. The appropriate outlet is *singing God's praise.* Someone once said that human beings "are naturally disposed to sing, because they wish to communicate their feelings. Speaking is the natural language of the understanding, and singing is the natural language of the heart."

Is anyone among you sick? Let him call for the elders of the church, and let them pray over him. In the New Testament, each church would strive to appoint a plural number of elders (Acts 14:23; 20:17) who would serve as spiritual shepherds in one local congregation (Acts 20:28; 1 Pet. 5:2). Hence, James speaks of *"the elders of the church."* So close is the relation of shepherd and sheep, that it is only natural for one who had become seriously ill to call for the elders, as spiritual mentors, to his bedside. Though the practice is often neglected in modern times, this is a situation in which elders should act in unison, visiting the ailing saint together and offering comfort and prayer on his or her behalf.

What are we to make of the next phrase in verse 14, *"anointing him with oil in the name of the Lord"*? Oil sometimes had medicinal uses (Luke 10:34), but "here its effect is not so much medicinal as symbolic, probably as a symbol of the protection and blessing of God on the patient" (DNTT, vol. 2, p. 712). The closest parallel in the New Testament is Mark 6:13, which describes the use of oil in miraculous healing. The pouring or smearing of olive oil had a long history in Jewish custom as a sign of God's special presence and good favor. In this way, God's prophets (Isa. 61:1), priests (Exod. 29:7), and kings (1 Sam. 10:1) were set apart for service.*

From A.D. 852 on, the Roman Catholic Church used this scripture to formally make Extreme Unction an official sacrament (a.k.a. the "Last Rites" or "Anointing of the Sick"), commonly administered at the end of a person's life. However, in James 5 the use of oil is to prepare a person for recovery, not for death. Moreover, it is "the elders of the church," not a special class of priests, who anoint the ailing. Finally, whatever soothing and symbolic properties belong to the oil, it is the "prayer of faith" that saves the sick, and the "Lord" who raises him up (v. 15). The oil, however important and comforting as an accompaniment, is secondary to prayer.

The Power of Prayer (5:15–16)

At first glance, many people recoil at the statement of verse 15. Surely James cannot be offering an unequivocal promise that *"the prayer of faith will save the one who is sick, and the Lord will raise him up"*—or can he? In the real world, the promise of forgiveness of sins at the end of the verse is easier to swallow than a guarantee of physical healing.

Consequently, some explain the whole passage as *spiritual healing,* devoid of any physical benefit. This seems to butcher the language somewhat, and to make the last part of verse 15 ("And if he has committed sins...") somewhat redundant. Others argue that James is speaking of *miraculous healing,* but the main point has to do with the power of prayer, not miracle-working. Elijah performed miracles, but he was "a man with a nature like ours," and it was his prayers rather than his miracles that affected the rain (vv. 17–18).

In any case, God does not always heal the sick. Paul left Trophimus sick at Miletus (2 Tim. 4:20), although he may have recovered in due

---

* For high-octane students, a fuller treatment of this issue can be found in Gary S. Shogren, "Will God Heal Us—A Re-examination of James 5:14–16a," *The Evangelical Quarterly* 61.2 (Apr.–June 1989): 99–108.

time. And Paul himself had a "thorn in the flesh," perhaps a physical ailment, which the Lord decided not to remove (2 Cor. 12:7–9). Ultimately, all men have an appointment with death (Heb. 9:27). On the other hand, God did give King Hezekiah an additional 15 years (2 Kings 20:1–6). And when King Asa sought help from physicians, refusing to seek the Lord, he died (2 Chron. 16:12).

Probably, it is best to view James 5:15 as a case in which James' eyes are on the general rule rather than all the exceptions (see the Power Point below). The connection of faith and prayer is made three times in James (1:6; 4:2–3; 5:14–18), and it is contrasted with double-mindedness (1:8; 4:8), with doubt (1:6), and with pleasure seeking (4:3). That said, all such prayers must be modified with the attitude, "not my will, but yours, be done" (*cf.* Luke 22:42). There comes a time when God knows best and for reasons that our higher than our own (Isa. 55:8–9), he decides not to grant a physical cure.

But have you ever stopped to consider how many prayers of healing God *does* answer in powerful ways? Do we realize how many people would have died without prayer? Is our "God" too small? The answer to prayer may not be immediate, so we must "wait on God" and continue earnestly in prayer. Over and over again, the scriptures remind us of God's powerful answers

POWER POINT

Some reasons why people do not recover from illness, from a spiritual point of view:

- Prayers are lacking in faith (James 1:6; 5:15)
- A higher purpose must be served (James 1:2–4; 2 Cor. 12:7–9)
- Sin (1 Cor. 11:30; John 5:14)
- Refusal to pray (James 4:2)
- No desire to get better (John 5:6)
- Poor health practices or foolish choices (Eph. 6:3)
- Refusal to pray according to God's will (1 John 5:14–15)

to prayer (Ps. 107:17–20; Mark 11:22–24; Eph. 3:20–21). God rewards the extraordinary faith of ordinary Christians. *He does heal the sick!* As Gary Shogren says of James 5, "The unspoken assumption is that if God does not heal, it will be out of the ordinary."

It is also clear from this passage that the ultimate goal is not physical healing but spiritual recovery (5:15b–16). This is reinforced in verses 19 and 20. Sometimes, but not always, there is a direct association between personal sin and physical illness (Ps. 32:3–4; 38:3; 1 Cor. 11:28–30; John 5:14). Serious illness also has a way of forcing people to examine and reorder their spiritual lives. That is why, when elders come to pray for physical healing, that confession and forgiveness of sins are so important. James uses language that points beyond physical life on earth to ultimate realities. Consequently, even when all hope for physical recovery is lost, the "prayer of faith" is still answered. When God is finally done with his faithful servants on earth, he will take us home to glory. What more could any saint ask for than that? *"The prayer of a righteous person has great power"*—not only because we witness a powerful God in action, but because fervency in prayer helps us focus on the bigger picture!

Elijah: An Example of the Power of Prayer (5:17–18)

Elijah was *a man just like us*—he was human! He was weak, just as we are weak. He became despondent, just as we become despondent. In fact, one might say he even suffered an emotional burnout (1 Kings 19:1–10). We tend to idealize the men and women of the Bible, but God's Word often describes their flaws along with their heroics.

But it is precisely because he had feet of clay that we have confidence to do what he did in the middle of a national crisis—*to pray*. Elijah first prayed that conditions would become worse before they got better. Most Israelites of the time, at the instigation of wicked Queen Jezebel, were Baal worshipers. In Canaanite mythology, Baal was a god associated with thunderstorms. However inconvenient, Elijah prayed for a drought! This would help people see Baal's impotence as a rain god. Then, after the great victory of the LORD God over Baal at Mt. Carmel (1 Kings 18), Elijah prayed for rain. Storm clouds suddenly appeared out of nowhere. It takes great faith to pray for a national calamity until spiritual conditions improve, but Elijah's prayers were answered! This is a marvelous example of what the "prayer of faith" can do.

The Power to Change an Eternal Destiny (5:19–20)

"My brothers, if anyone among you wanders from the truth and someone brings him back, let him know that whoever brings back a sinner from his wandering will save his soul from death and will cover a multitude of sins." These are the last words in the Letter of James and a fitting end. In a great fireworks display, there is often a "grand finale." Yet what could be a grander "finale" than impacting a brother's eternal destiny for good?

On my office wall stands a beautiful composite portrait, summarizing 16 years my family and I had contributed to the Lord's work in Tustin, California. The painstaking artwork was a gift by a talented brother, Gary McDonald. During most of our time in Southern California, Gary had been an erring Christian who had lapsed back into the world. On a few pivotal occasions, I had bumped into him and struck up an acquaintance. After learning about his condition, I encouraged him to return to God and to "get serious" about it. I really didn't do much to help Gary, but my simple words made a powerful impression on him. After he repented and came back to the Lord, he never forgot, periodically reminding me how those words of encouragement had changed his life. Gary is gone now, the victim of lung cancer, but he died full of faith and hope. The portrait is a lingering reminder of what can happen when we take an interest in lost souls. Our labor is "not in vain" in the Lord (1 Cor. 15:58).

Summary

We face various crises in life. Certainly, there are physical (5:13–15), spiritual (5:15–16), national (5:17–18), and eternal (5:19–20) dimensions involved. When a Christian is deeply connected to God, and constant in prayer, he should never underestimate the potential for good that he has in this wicked world. God can use each of us to make a difference. We must open our eyes to the opportunities all around us, and then take the initiative. When we depend on God every step of the way, the Lord will work through us in powerful ways.

REINFORCING THE LESSON

1. Verses 13 and 14 remind us that there is an appropriate spiritual response to every condition of life. What happens when we fail to plug into the right spiritual outlet at a critical time?

2. What is the main point James makes about prayer in this section?

3. In order for the physically ill to call for "the elders of the church" during a health crisis, there must be a certain rapport with the elders as *spiritual shepherds*. What are some things that will contribute to a healthy relationship with the elders prior to the onset of a crisis?

4. Thought question: when elders pray for the sick today, should they bring a vial of olive oil with them, or should this be viewed simply as an ancient Jewish custom?

5. Elijah prayed for a drought (v. 17). Is it ever appropriate for modern Christians to pray for hard times during a national crisis?

6. What must be done to "bring someone back" from spiritual error? 5:19–20

Epistle of James

What makes life dreary is absence of motive. What makes life complicated is multiplicity of motive. What makes life victorious is singleness of motive.
—*George Eliot*

1. James calls himself a _____ of God and the Lord Jesus Christ.

2. James addresses this letter to the twelve tribes in the _____.

3. At the outset, James urges us to count it all _____ when we encounter various _____.

4. Let no one say when he is tempted, "I am being _____ by God," for God cannot be tempted with evil, and he himself tempts no one.

5. Each person is tempted when he is lured and enticed by his own _____.

6. Be _____ of the word, and not _____ only, deceiving yourselves.

7. Has not God chosen those who are _____ in the world to be _____ in faith and heirs of the kingdom?

8. So speak and so act as those who are to be judged under the law of _____. For judgment is without mercy to one who has shown no _____.

9. For as the body apart from the spirit is dead, so also _____ apart from _____ is dead.

10. No human being can tame the _____. It is a restless evil, full of deadly _____.

11. The wisdom _____ _____ is first pure, then peaceable, gentle, open to reason, full of mercy and good fruits, impartial and sincere.

12. Whoever wishes to be a _____ of the world makes himself an _____ of God.

13. So whoever knows the right thing to do and fails to do it, for him it is _____.

14. Be patient, therefore, brothers, until the _____ of the Lord.

15. Is anyone among you suffering? Let him _____.
Is anyone cheerful? Let him _____ _____.
Is anyone among you sick? Let him call for the _____ of the church, and let them pray over him.

16. Whoever brings back a sinner from his wandering will save his soul from _____ and will cover a _____ of sins.

More Bible workbooks that you can order from Spiritbuilding.com or your favorite Christian bookstore.

Inside Out (Carl McMurray)
Studying spiritual growth in bite sized pieces
Night and Day (Andrew Roberts)
Comparing N.T. Christianity and Islam
Church Discipline (Royce DeBerry)
A quarter's study on an important task for the church
Exercising Authority (John Baughn)
How we use and understand authority on a daily basis
Compass Points (Carl McMurray)
22 foundation lessons for home studies or new Christians
We're Different Because... (Carl McMurray)
workbook on authority and recent church history that ought to be taught regularly
Communing with the Lord (Matthew Allen)
A study of the Lord's Supper and issues surrounding it
From Beneath the Altar (Carl McMurray)
A workbook commentary on the book of Revelation
Marriage Through the Ages (Royce & Cindy DeBerry)
A quarter's study of God's design for this part of our life
Parenting Through the Ages (Royce & Cindy DeBerry)
Bible principles tested and explained by successful parents
1 & 2 Timothy and Titus (Matthew Allen)
A workbook commentary on these letters from Paul
The Parables, Taking a Deeper Look (Kipp Campbell)
A relevant examination of our Lord's teaching stories
The Minor Prophets, Vol. 1 & 2 (Matthew Allen)
Old lessons that speak directly to us today
Esteemed of God, Studying the Book of Daniel (Carl McMurray)
Covering the man as well as the time between the testaments
What Should I Do? (Dennis Tucker)
A study that seeks Bible answers to life's important questions

Reveal In Me... (Jeanne Sullivan)
A ladies study on finding and developing one's own talents
I Will NOT Be Lukewarm, Ppt/Teacher's Manual (Dana Burk)
A ladies study on defeating mediocrity
The Gospel of John (Cassondra Givans)
A study for women, by a woman, on this letter of John
Sisters at War (Cassondra Givans)
Breaking the generation gap between sisters in Christ
Will You Wipe My Tears? (Joyce Jamerson)
Resources to teach us how to help others through sorrow
Bridges or Barriers, w/Manual (Cindy DeBerry/Angie Kmitta)
Study encouraging harmony with younger/older sisters-in-Christ
Learning to Sing at Midnight (Joanne Beckley)
A study book about spiritual growth benefiting women of all ages

Transitions, with Ppt/Teacher's Manual (Ken Weliever)
A relevant life study for this changing age group
Snapshots: Defining Moments in a Girl's Life (Nicole Sardinas)
How to make godly decisions when it really matters
The Path of Peace (Cassondra Givans)
Relevant and important topics of study for teens
The Purity Pursuit (Andrew Roberts)
Helping teens achieve purity in all aspects of life
Paul's Letter to the Romans (Matthew Allen)
Putting righteousness by faith on an understandable level

It's Not About Me: Becoming an A+ Teacher (Ed Major)
Workbook for teaching adults how to teach the Bible to adults
AUTISM, In the Eye of the Hurricane (Juli Liske)
A family's journey from the shock of an autistic diagnosis to victory
For However Brief a Time (Warren Berkley)
A son's human interest tales of his father in a time now gone by

CPSIA information can be obtained at www.ICGtesting.com
Printed in the USA
LVOW05s2100070214

372806LV00003B/32/P